BLESS 'EM ALL!

Life in the Women's Land Army
at Lubenham, Leicestershire

Pat Fox

BLESS 'EM ALL!

Life in the Women's Land Army at Lubenham, Leicestershire

Pat Fox

Market Harborough Historical Society

BLESS 'EM ALL!
Life in the Women's Land Army
at Lubenham, Leicestershire

Pat Fox

ISBN 978-0-9557686-1-3

Published by
Market Harborough Historical Society

Market Harborough Historical Society
Harborough Museum, Council Offices, Adam & Eve Street
Market Harborough, LE16 7AG

Designed by Heart of Albion
Printed in England by Booksprint

Contents

List of illustrations

Acknowledgements

Grateful thanks to Market Harborough and The Bowdens Charity, Frank Hargreave, Pam Aucott, Jane Tugwell and colleagues at Market Harborough Museum, David Carter, Sheila Coates, Eve Fox, Barbara Johnson and Colin Sullivan.

Introduction

Women's Land Army

Much has been written on the military aspects of the Second World War, but the home front has been relatively neglected as a subject for study. While troops, airmen and sailors were directly engaged in fighting the enemy, there was another battle being waged in the factories and fields which was also of great importance. War had become 'total' affecting everyone much more directly than any previous war. Everyone was in the front line in some form or function.

Our fighting men and the civilian population needed supplies and the war in the Atlantic made the import of material and foodstuffs difficult. Britain had to become more self sufficient in these areas.

An additional challenge was that many who had previously worked in predominantly male preserves had been drafted into the armed forces. Into the breach stepped thousands of women taking up occupations not only in munitions factories and production work of all kinds but also replacing men in farming occupations.

Women had responded to the needs of the country in the First World War and thousands had volunteered to carry out work in hospitals, factories (including the famous 'Canary girls' undertaking dangerous work in munitions plants) and in all spheres of public and commercial life including, for the first time, the armed services. Their efforts undoubtedly enabled victory for the allied forces.

The Second World War was more all consuming and for the first time the whole civilian population was influenced by war with many being in the front line during bombing raids and the Blitz. Such was the totality of war that for the first time women were forcibly conscripted into essential war work. Although with the threat of war in the late 1930s women were volunteering in considerable numbers for roles in the Fire Service, Red Cross, Auxiliary Hospital services, and various ARP (Air Raid Precautions) organisations, there were still not enough women to bridge the gap left by conscripted men as the war got underway. Thus on 18th December 1941 Parliament reluctantly passed the National Services Act (No. 2) and by February 1942 all women aged between eighteen and sixty, married or single with or without children, had to register with the Ministry of Labour. Single and childless women were often sent to other parts of the country and Pat Fox moved willingly from her family home in Eckington, seven miles south of Sheffield, to Lubenham.

Pat's experiences in the Women's Land Army (WLA) gives a valuable and lively account of what it was like to be part of a movement that contributed incalculably to allied victory. The WLA had its origins in the First World War and was a way of filling labour shortages in agricultural work. Ominous war clouds in the late 1930s led to the re-formation of a number of voluntary organisations in preparation for the inevitable conflict, including the WLA, later to be dubbed 'The Land Girls'. The organisation was re-constituted under the honorary directorship of Lady Denham, whose home at Balcombe Place was made its general headquarters.

England and Wales were divided for administrative purposes into seven regions with a regional officer in charge of an inspection team. Each county had its own WLA office, the one in Leicestershire being based in Leicester. Most prospective Land Girls were interviewed at county level. Pat Fox was unusual in that she was interviewed at her local office in Sheffield but had requested to move to Lubenham to be with her friend who had begun work there in 1940. As Pat states, training could be comprehensive or cursory, depending on the farmers' and other agricultural workers' attitudes. Pat certainly learned a lot of skills, such as driving a tractor and gained considerable knowledge of agricultural work and life.

In comparison to other Land Girls Pat had a lengthy career in WLA which spanned both war and peace times. This gives us some insight into the changing attitudes to, for example, prisoners of war. In her account she reveals how everyone, be they American, German, Italian or British were ordinary human beings who found themselves in extraordinary circumstances. She reminisces about the acts of kindness shown by people on all sides in this unfortunate conflict. She also reveals the spirit of camaraderie among the girls in the WLA hostel in Lubenham.

She graphically explains the hard work in often difficult conditions which the 'girls' had to endure. She was sometimes hungry, the work was often dangerous (she sustained work injuries on several occasions) and the pay and remuneration were not generous. Women were paid far less than men for doing the same jobs. She also experienced tragedy when her American fiancée was killed in France and she poignantly describes receiving letters and parcels from his mother.

She also gives a good account of the activities of the Land Girls in peace time. Despite the ending of the war, rationing and shortages continued, and having won the war the civilian population, including the returning troops, had to 'win the peace'. This meant boosting exports to pay for the war and to rebuild a war torn economy. In fact the conditions in the immediate post-war years, especially in the 'freeze up' of the winter 1946 and 1947 were in many ways harder than during the war.

By the end of the 1940s things had gradually begun to improve and more and more provisions were removed from rationing. Returning demobilised men once more began to take over the jobs that women had occupied, and Pat mentions the move towards being employed 'private' in the latter stages of the Land Army's existence. Many of the women, including Pat, met local men, got married and turned to a more domesticated life as housewives and mothers. The WLA was finally wound up in 1950.

Many of the women like Pat and those in other accounts referred to at the end of this introduction, found a rich and rewarding experience in making a contribution to the war and some resented the return to a more sedate life. Others were glad to settle back into domesticity satisfied that they had made their best contribution towards 'digging for victory'. One thing is for certain that had it not been for the contribution of Pat and the thousands of women like her, Britain could not have prosecuted an effective war.

Enjoy this informative and entertaining account of one of those women who served their country well.

Dr Len Holden

Secretary, Market Harborough Historical Society

Pat Fox in 1944, soon after joining the Women's Land Army.

Eckington, Derbyshire in about 1950.
Pat's home in Church Row faces the church tower.

My Family and Early Life

My family lived in a village named Eckington, which lies seven miles from Sheffield in one direction and seven miles from Chesterfield in the other, although we were actually in the county of Derbyshire. Most of the men in the village worked as coalminers in one or other of the four local pits.

We lived in Church Row near to the church. Our house was one of fifteen houses that were on a bank along side the River Moss. Further on there was a plantation leading to a flourmill and woods.

We were a family of ten children and I was thirteen years old when the Second World War began. Father had fought in the First World War and was in the Territorials – The Sherwood Foresters. The Government could see trouble ahead and father was called up a couple months prior to the outbreak of war. My sister Lily was married on Saturday, 2nd September 1939 and war was declared next day. Father was given a few hours off duty to give Lily away at her wedding.

I left school in December as I was now fourteen years old and able to go to work. My eldest sister Edith was already married and lived in Middleton on the far side of Manchester. Her husband had been called up for the Navy. Being as she was alone, I went to live with her and she found me a job in a cotton mill. I stayed there until I was nearly seventeen years old.

When I returned home I got a temporary job until I decided what I wanted to do. My eldest brother Harry had served a five-year apprenticeship in the steel works in Chesterfield. He was called up and became a mechanic in the RAF. Gladys, one of my older sisters, joined the Women's Auxiliary Air Force (WAAF). Bette, two years younger than me, when she was old enough joined the Women's Auxiliary Territorial Service (ATS). I think we all wanted to help in whatever way we could towards the war effort.

Joining the Women's Land Army

I had thought of joining the Women's Land Army (WLA). My mother's friend invited me to tea one Saturday because her daughter, Betty, was in the WLA and was coming home for the weekend bringing another girl along with her. I went along to have a chat and get some information about the work involved. They were at Lubenham Hostel, near Market Harborough, Leicestershire. Having made up my mind, I caught a bus into Sheffield

The author (in front) with her sisters Gladys (left) and Nora (centre) and their friend Eva Bluff (right).

Three of the posters issued to recruit volunteers for the Women's Land Army.

to go to the Recruiting Office, where I was asked all kinds of questions, then told I would have to have a medical examination. I asked "If I pass, could I go to Lubenham Hostel." "Where's that?" they enquired, never having heard of it. I told them that it was in Leicestershire. As Betty was there and I had met her friend Rene (Ginger) I thought at least I'd know someone there! Betty only stayed twelve months.

I passed my medical and my uniform duly arrived together with my travel warrant. As from 29th April 1943 to 18th March 1950, I was a member of the WLA, number 121483.

I left home on the Monday morning and caught a bus into Sheffield for the railway station, changing trains at Derby, Leicester and Market Harborough, finally arriving late afternoon at Lubenham Station. Walking down the path, after directions from the station porter, I was met by a Land Girl, who had been sent to meet me. We walked round the village green to the hostel, where I was introduced to the warden in charge of the hostel, also to Margaret, my first forewoman there – a lovely person.

The hostel was purpose-built for the girls. It was 'T'-shaped and on the right-hand side it was brick built for the ablution block, containing four bathrooms, six washbasins, six toilets, a boiler-room, which apart from the huge water boiler, had rails around the sides for we girls to dry our wet clothes or washing. To the left was a huge wooden dormitory divided into cubicles, each sleeping four girls, on thin wooden slatted bunks, with

Women's Land Army cap badge.

Lubenham railway station.
Courtesy David Carter.

two bunks either side of the cubicle. Below this was an office for the forewoman and private bedroom. There was also a room for the assistant cook. Along from the front door was a large dining room with a serving hatch to the large kitchen. Beyond that were bedrooms for the warden, under-warden and cook, with a private sitting room adjacent. In both the dormitory and dining room were two combustion stoves set in a square of concrete. This was all the heating we had and with concrete floors, you can well imagine how cold it was in winter.

Working in the Welland Valley

By spring 1940, two million fresh acres had gone under the plough. We now had to grow our own grains that had previously been imported. Here in Lubenham, we were in the Welland Valley well known for beef cattle. Being mostly grassland, many of the farmers did not own a tractor. A War Agriculture Committee was set up in all districts. Ours was on St Mary's Road in Market Harborough. Farmers would apply to the office to ask for us girls and in most instances stating how many days we were needed and the kind of work we would be doing. The Labour Officer would then contact our forewoman and she would tell us where we were allocated to. The farmers were paying the office six shillings a day for a girl; at the end of the week our pay was fourteen shillings.

Girls came in all shapes and sizes. I'm sure some of them wondered what they had let themselves in for as most of them had been working in shops, offices or factories on sewing machines. My brother told me I would not stick it three weeks when I started pulling mangolds in the frosty weather, but I did! I have read some books where some of the WLA said they had been sent to this specialised farm or college to be taught a craft or milking. No such thing at our place. We were sent to a farm and, if we didn't know what to do, the farmer or one of his men would show us for a little while and then leave us to get on with it. The only job we did not do was lift the huge railway sacks that were fastened to the back of the threshing drum, as these sacks held either two-and-a-quarter hundredweight (115 kg) of wheat, two hundredweight of barley (100 kg) or one-and-a-half hundredweight of oats (76 kg), depending on which crop we were working. There was nothing else we could not tackle, and we did everything in its season.

The forewoman came round each night to tell you where you were working the next day, that is, unless you were put on a gang for certain jobs. How well I remember my first job!

Land Girls and farm workers taking a break from threshing.
Left to right: unknown man, Maria Sullivan, Dorothy Adcock, unknown Land Girl, Paddy Donahue, Jean Frost and Albert Corton (drum boss).
Photograph taken by the author.

Threshing

My first job was to go with a gang threshing. It was a hard task and you got filthy each day. We were given heavy khaki bicycles and often had to ride ten miles to work. Otherwise we went in an open lorry, and were dropped at isolated fields and picked up each evening. We girls were mostly given a Threshing Boss; he would

be in sole charge of tractor and threshing drum. When we had finished threshing at one farm, we would clean down and sheet down the machine, then we moved on to the next farm. We did this most winters. One girl would be the bandcutter and another the feeder, feeding the loose sheaves onto the beaters. This would separate the wheat from the chaff, the corn coming out at the back into hessian sacks, which would hold two-and-a-quarter hundredweight of grain. Chaff coming out at the front onto the floor between the drum and elevator had to be moved well away from the machine

Land Army girls on the threshing machine, Gumley. Photograph taken by the author.

and was a dirty job, so we all took turns on this task. Other girls would be pitching sheaves up to the drum. We all enjoyed working together.

This job we did from late October as some of the farmers were needing corn to feed cattle throughout the winter or taken to the market for sale. Once we were working at a farm just outside the village of Tur Langton for Mr R.A. Wadland. The machine had stopped as corn had backed up inside it. Victor Chandler, the boss, got underneath the machine and let all the corn out onto the floor, started the machine, then told me to get underneath and clean it all up into sacks.

"While the machine is going?" I asked.

"Yes, you'll be alright if you keep your head down" was the reply.

I filled one sack lying on my tummy, did the next sack and was coming out from underneath and evidently came up too soon, and felt an almighty thump on the back of my head. I called to the girls working on the drum "Who's throwing up there?"

"No one," came the reply. I had come up too soon and hit my head on the huge driving belt. Fortunately this was on the flat side of the belt, not the edge of it. Even so, my head was cut open. I had to walk back to the village to ask the farmer's wife to take me into Market Harborough to see the doctor, where I had part of my hair cut away and three stitches inserted. I was then put on the sick list for two weeks. The farmer's wife took me back to the hostel. What price health and safety?

Threshing beans at one place was a bit hard. The beans have very thick tough stalks. When trying to pitchfork the sheaves to the drum you would find they got entwined in neighbouring sheaves and would not budge. Also these had been stacked damp so there were mildew stalks. We coughed, sneezed and spluttered and though winter, we washed our faces in a nearby stream before we cycled back to the hostel.

A Dirty Job

At another farm, whilst we were threshing in the ice and snow, the boss sent me to the farmhouse at dinner time for a can of tea. It wasn't quite ready so I had a look round the yard buildings, finally going into the cowshed. There I saw a land girl cleaning up and hosing down, but she was covered in wet cow muck. I asked her "Whatever have you done?" She said that she had to shovel everything up into the wheelbarrow and take it out to the muckle (muck dump) in the yard. This involved wheeling the barrow up a narrow plank and tipping it on top of the muckle. However, being snowy and icy, the wheelbarrow had slipped off the plank and she had gone with it. Needless to say she was covered from head to toe in sloppy cow muck. She told me she was going to pack it in as she was in lodgings in the village and was lonely. "Don't do that," I said, "you're in Leicestershire, phone the Head Office in Leicester and ask for a transfer to the Lubenham Hostel. You will like it there. There are forty of us girls. There is always someone in during the evening and we make our own entertainment." She did and eventually turned up at the hostel, where she stayed until she married in 1948.

Lunch Breaks

Another time our gang was threshing peas in the village of Gumley, working alongside Italian prisoners. The POW camp was not too far away on Farndon Road in Market Harborough. It was winter with snow on the ground. The Italian sergeant used to build a nice fire each day, well away from the stacks of peas, so we could have a warm at break time. This particular sergeant would come round saying "You have five minutes break," and he would take over your job whilst you had a rest. There was a stream in the field, so, each evening he would take some threshed dried

Farm workers and Land Army girls with Albert Corton.

peas and soak them overnight in a tin. Then the next day they were put onto the fire in a can to cook. It didn't matter what you had in your sandwiches – bread and jam or beetroot, we all ate peas with them. Believe me, the work was so hard we worked up great appetites and would eat practically anything.

On another occasion, we were threshing out at the far side of Husbands Bosworth and we had finished for the day; I was so hungry that my legs felt like jelly. I asked Charlie Wormleighton, the drum boss, if he had any food left. He always came to work with half a loaf (there was no butter) and a wedge of cheese. He had a bit of dry bread left which was none too clean, as Charlie, being in charge, used to go round at regular intervals oiling the grease nipples on the machinery and some of it got on the bread, but I was so hungry I ate the bread before attempting to cycle back the seven miles to the hostel.

I had never ridden a bike before coming to the hostel and one day I had to cycle into Market Harborough. We were threshing opposite the prisoner of war camp. I didn't know how to stop the bike as there were no brakes, so I slowed down as much as possible on the grass verge and promptly fell off. It was lovely having the prisoners laughing at me! I also fell off the bike down Lubenham Hill the same day coming back to the hostel from which I suffered two lovely sore knees.

Rats!

We were required by law to put wire netting round the stacks as we got further down towards the base. This was in the hope of catching rats. As an island, Britain had to be self-sufficient as very few food ships were able to get through to us. Therefore every grain had to be preserved from the rats and other vermin.

We'd have one person pitching sheaves into the drum, with the rest of the gang at the ready with sticks and pitchforks to kill any rats they could see. This had to be done as the rats would nest in the stacks, gnawing the string binding the sheaves and apart from making such a mess they were eating all the corn. One girl at another hostel told me a rat jumped off the stack onto the back of her neck before jumping to the ground. She said she can still feel it when she thinks about it! At another farm we went to, we had the wire netting round and as we got lower on the stack, we could feel it moving beneath our feet. I was pitching sheaves up to the drum, everyone stood around ready armed with sticks etc. Believe it or not, that day we killed and put into the wheelbarrow over two hundred rats. Ugh! In one area you could get sixpence a tail for each rat you caught, but not in our area!

Time Sheets

We girls were given time sheets for the week and had to take them with us to work and get them signed at the end of each day by the farmer. If they were not signed we would not receive any money for the day, even if we'd worked. Needless to say we made sure we got them signed! One farmer was never nice to the girls. None of us liked him. Threshing a couple of wheat stacks for him meant very hard work for us but we kept going. The reason for this was that we wanted to get away from this farm. Having finished, the other four girls asked me to take the time sheets to the farmer to sign. Sometimes he would say "I haven't time now, come round to the house tonight". However, he said "Yes, I'll sign them. You've been very good girls and worked very hard". I said "Thank you" and he replied "I'm so pleased with you I am going to give you a tip". Again I thanked him and going back to the girls I repeated what he had said. O lovely, how much has he given us. Two and sixpence (half a crown) between the five of us! That meant sixpence each. Said Paddy "By Jesus that's not enough to buy us half a pint" – half a pint of beer or shandy was sixpence halfpenny.

Prisoners of War

One September time I picked a few blackberries after I'd eaten lunch. An Italian POW who was quite elderly worked on the farm of Mr Tony Oakey on a regular basis. He came to me and said "Come, we pick some willow canes". Having gathered these, he laid them in a stream weighted down with stones, saying "tomorrow you sit with me at dinner time". So next day, having eaten our sandwiches, we fetched the willow canes out of the

stream and the Italian wove me a lovely basket. Giving it to me he said " Now you pick blackberries."

On another occasion a Labour Officer came to the hostel and told me he would pick me up in the mornings in a small van for a couple of weeks, as he wanted me as feeder and band cutter on this threshing drum. When the drum boss arrived, a stranger to me, there I was working with him and eight German POWs. I must say they were all quite nice to me and polite. One day an older one approached me at dinner time

Italian POWs picking potatoes in 1944. Courtesy Leicestershire Museums Service.

A POW harvesting on a Lubenham farm using an early combine harvester. The author also drove similar machinery. Courtesy Leicestershire Museums Service.

bringing with him a young lad of no more than nineteen years. The young lad had made a toy in wood, similar to a table tennis bat. On this bat were four little chickens carved in the wood. Here and there little marks had been burnt into the bat to look like grains of wheat. Attached to the chickens was string which went through four small holes. Pulling the string from underneath it seemed as though the chickens were pecking the grain. Would I like to buy it? How much are you asking for it? The young lad did not speak any English so it was the older man who opened the young one's jacket showing

Tractor bogged down.
Courtesy Leicestershire Museums Service.

me that the boy's trousers were held up with string. He would like a belt – I told him I could not get one till Montag (Monday). The only time I had off was Saturday afternoon and Sunday. I asked my forewoman if she would buy a belt for me. She asked me why I needed a belt when I already had one. Explaining the reason, she got me one and I was able to pay the young man, who was quite overcome with his new belt.

One morning arriving for work, I was longing to 'spend a penny'. Looking around I thought, "Good, the boss had not arrived and no Germans in sight" so I relieved myself. Quite near the workplace, redressing myself, suddenly a voice said " Guten Morgen (Good morning)" . Yes, the Germans were there already, sat on top of the straw stack to keep warm till we began work. I just called "Good Morning" and got on with oiling the threshing drum.

New Girls

Quite a few girls were from Leicester, the rest of us mostly from Derbyshire and Sheffield. I did not go home too often as I couldn't afford the fare. One Sunday the warden in charge of the hostel asked if I would go into Market Harborough to meet six new girls who were coming from Sheffield on this particular Sunday. I duly met the girls at the railway station and escorted them into the Square to catch a bus to Lubenham. (The buses go from a new bus station these days.) I told them I would pay their fare today: six at one penny each. Tomorrow it is going up to tuppence (two old pence)..

Next day, one of the girls was put on our threshing gang. The boss said she was to go on the 'pulse' (beans etc) or 'chaff' as we called it. I said "No! it's a filthy job". So our new girl went onto the stack and was taught how to use a pitchfork. Most of the stacks had been thatched against the weather. These were bundles or battens of straw gathered and straightened tidily into bundles, then laid in rows overlapping each other, pegged down with thatch pegs, sticks that were pointed and plunged into batten and stack, then string fastened along to keep them tight. On a new job, the first thing to do was to climb to the apex of the stack to undo all this to get to get to the sheaves. At one farm we had some English soldiers working with us. The farmer asked one of the soldiers to go on to the roof to do this job. He said he was frightened of heights. Guess who got the job?

On one occasion when threshing in Foxton Village, we girls walked across a ploughed field to the stack in the bottom corner, when Margaret tripped and severely hurt her ankle. One of the Italian POWs went to the farmhouse to ask if the farmer would take her to our local cottage hospital, which he did and I also went with her. Fortunately the ankle was not broken but very badly sprained, so she was off farm work for a week. Another time we were threshing just outside Foxton village for another farmer and on the second morning we went to work only to find an airman on guard at the field gate, holding a rifle. We were not going to be allowed in as a plane had crashed in the field. The drum boss spoke to him and a second airman got through to the aerodrome just up the road. Shortly we were able to go into the field to get on with our work. Another time out at Langton, the machine had broken down, the weather was so cold we girls were stamping our feet and blowing our hands in order to keep warm. The next thing I remember was coming round to find myself lying in the hay. I had fainted outside in the cold, so a chappie carried me into the barn to get warm.

One day we were in a shepherd's hut at lunchtime, as it was a very cold winters day. There was a fireplace in this hut and we had a fire going. A young lad, John Smallbones, had just left school at fourteen years of age and this was his first job on the farm. He pulled up a box close to the fire to warm himself and one of the German POWs moved him away from the fire. John moved back near the fire again. The German moved him back again. This happened three times and poor little John burst into tears. I said to the German "Why don't you leave him alone?" He replied that it wasn't good for the boy to get too warm only to go outside into the cold again otherwise he would never grow into an old man.

Accidents!

On one occasion we were sent threshing at Debdale near Kibworth, working for Mr Ted Hulland. He was one of the nicest people to work for and certainly the most jovial. You could hear his loud laughter in the next field. We'd finished there and were moving on to the next farm only a couple of fields away near the canal. Ted had a pony and trap and he told us we could load the scales, which were large, into the trap. Sylvia and I did this and the three of us got into the trap. I asked Ted if I could take the reins. I'd never done this before, but he agreed and taking the reins I cried "Gee up", the pony did a jump and driving the trap up a gated road I turned to ask Ted if everything was OK only to find he was lying in the roadway. We'd started off so quickly Ted had lost his balance and fallen out of the trap. Poor Ted!

Fred, who was working with us at the same farm had a small green car with a canvas hood. He gave us a ride in the car at lunchtime. I asked if he'd teach me to drive. Taking the wheel, we set off but hadn't gone many yards when we finished up in the ditch. No one hurt and no damage to the car as I was going slowly.

Spring Sowing

Some farmers would start ploughing straight after harvest if the weather was fit to plant wheat and oats. They would also sow seed in spring for a later crop, also in spring plant sugar beet, mangolds and swedes. These would be done using a broad seed drill, mostly drawn by horses, but tractors were becoming more popular. Those farmers who hadn't one

could hire one from the War Agricultural Board along with a driver. Potatoes were set by hand. There would be full sacks put down the furrows. Then we would fill our buckets and walk up one furrow, then down the next row by row, dropping one potato each step as we put one foot in front of the other. We would later on hoe and single where necessary all these root crops. On one occasion Elsie, my mate, and I were sent to a village seven miles away to hoe and single out a large field of cabbage plants. The farmer was a nice old gentleman who lived with his two unmarried sisters. He showed us the field, enquiring if we had done this before. We said

The author, an unknown Land Girl, Kay Conner and Avril Webb outside the Hostel in 1944.

Margaret Altobelli, Ida Harwood (forewoman), two unknown Land Girls and Jean Bale (kneeling) in the Hostel garden.

we had not. He showed us how and then left us to it. Next day we were there again and finished a little early so went to the house to get our timesheets signed. He said he was pleased with us and asked us if we would like to help ourselves to some strawberries from the garden? We enthusiastically replied, "Yes please!"

When hoeing and singling out crops, we would have to take care in some fields where plovers (peewits) were nesting and had laid their eggs. These birds nest in soil, not grass, hay or hedgerows, so we'd carefully go round them so as not to disturb the nest.

Betty West, unknown Land Girl, Sally Smith and Ruby Wells outside the Hostel.

Market Harborough and Stolen Bicycles

Welland Park in Market Harborough was also brought into the war effort and had to grow vegetables in what had been flower beds. I think these vegetables went to the local hospitals. Four of us were working there and during that time we made friends with a couple of young boys at the neighbouring school. I think they would be about twelve years old, and they would call for a chat at dinner time. One day, one of the boys called and said "We didn't think you were here as your cycles were not in the usual place". We thought the boys were playing a trick on us, but no, the cycles had vanished. My cycle and my mate's had gone, together with our haversacks that contained our lunches. We informed the park keeper who in turn called the police. The policeman asked how much the cycles were worth. Then asked how much the haversacks, the Thermos flask and sandwiches were worth. I gave him an estimate of the value. "What was in them – ham?" He asked. "You've got to be joking," I said. "Two bread and dripping, and one bread and piccalilli". Our two cycles were found a few days later in Coventry. Apparently two boys had absconded from a remand home, seen the bikes and pinched them. The cycles were sent back by train but the haversacks had been ditched.

Food

The food at the hostel was on the whole not too bad, but sandwich fillings were dreadful – beetroot and more beetroot, cucumber that had been placed in water overnight to keep it moist, meant we had lovely soggy sandwiches at midday. After chatting amongst ourselves we did a dreadful thing. We went on strike as we hadn't got very far speaking to the warden or under-warden. So we hitchhiked to Leicester to the *Leicester Mercury* offices, and we explained the situation to a reporter. The headline

next day was "Treat us as well as you do the Italians". They would come to work with a tin of John West salmon between two of them. From then on lunch packs did improve.

In the Hostel garden.
Back row: Margaret Altobelli with
two unknown land Army girls.
Front row: Jean Bale and Molly.

Jean Bale and the author relaxing on a haystack at Tin House Farm, Welham Lane, Great Bowden in 1945.

Hay Making

At some farms, during haymaking and harvesting, the farmer's wife would send us tea and sandwiches at teatime if we were working late, otherwise, we only had what we had taken with us. Haymaking was a lovely job, even if it was hard work. Some grass was cut by horse-drawn knife, others by tractor. The knife was really a long bar with triangular teeth through which the blade ran forwards and backwards cutting the hay into nice swathes. Everyone would pray that the weather kept fine. Two or three girls and other farm staff would go along the straight swaths turning the hay over so that the bottom hay was now on top to dry in the sun. It was hard work as all we had were pitchforks to work with. Perhaps the following day we would gather up the hay into haycocks (small domes of hay) or into larger cobs. These were then put onto carts or trailers, then taken to either a corner of the field or to a barn, then pitched up on to stacks, to be kept for winter feed. A lovely job, if tiring!

Harvesting

After haymaking which was usually done in June, came harvesting. The standing corn, oats or barley were mostly cut in earlier years by men using a scythe which they would keep sharp with a sharpening stone. Then came more tractors, so there would be machines which could cut the corn. These had sails going round pushing the corn into bundles and tying them up, and at the same time throwing the sheaves out in straight rows. Then along came a gang of girls who would pick up two sheaves at a time and place eight sheaves together to form a wigwam shape, setting them firmly into the ground. These were left a few days to dry in the sun. They were then loaded up onto a horse and cart or tractor and trailer, all being lifted with pitchforks.

More Accidents!

At one farm I'd been sent from the yard to the fields to get the two cart horses in, have their collars and tackle put on and positioned into the cart shafts ready for loading up the sheaves. The six German POWs who were to help us were already at the barns and had started to tackle up. I pointed out that they had got the wrong harness on the horses and that we would have to take it all off and start again. "No, just take off the blinkers and collar" said one. Believe me, blinkers are used for a purpose, so that the horse can only see in front. The German took these off one of the horses despite my protest, and the next thing the horse went berserk seeing the cart behind him and went galloping off through two fields. He then turned around came back down the field smashing through a hedge onto Foxton Road. It then went running up towards the aerodrome. The farmer was most angry and I was told off.

Working for this same farmer, I was driving a grey Ferguson tractor, with him on the cutter and binder. We had to stop for some reason, I went to get off the tractor but my trouser leg was caught fast on the footrest. I got back on to release my trouser leg but all this time my leg had been pulled back onto the exhaust pipe which ran along the side of the tractor. I didn't say anything to the boss as I knew he wanted to finish the field that night. When at the end of the day I was back at the hostel I showed my leg to the warden who immediately sent me to the cottage hospital in Market Harborough. My leg was attended to and I was put on sick leave for ten days, so I decided to go home to Eckington and our village doctor came each day to put fresh dressings on my leg. I still have a pretty white patch on the back of my leg where the burnt skin came off.

A Very Long Day

On another occasion, we were working for Mr B. Ashton at Hallaton. We were well away from the farmhouse stooking corn in a very large field. The farmer told the lorry driver Jock Murray that he need not pick the girls up tonight, as he wanted them to finish the field and that he would take them home. At 5 p.m. the other lorry came for the Italian POWs to take them back to camp. We girls plodded on stooking, not forgetting that we had double summertime and daylight until very late. We finally finished the field and went out to sit on the grass verge waiting for our lift. No joy! Eventually I said it would be nearer to walk into the next village, Slawston, than walk back to Hallaton. This we did and called at another farm asking the farmer if he would phone Mr Ashton and explain we were still waiting to be picked up. He duly arrived saying "I am awfully sorry girls I had forgotten all about you." We were so important to him he'd forgotton us! It was 11 p.m. when we got back to the hostel. The warden, Miss Corner, who was very nice, said "I've kept your dinner warm," but none of us wanted it as it had been dished up since 6.30 p.m. She also told us to be quiet as we got ready for bed as the rest of the girls were in their bunks asleep. We said that's where would like to be as well! We had had nothing to eat since we ate our two or three sandwiches at midday and were worn out. So we had a quick bath and collapsed in bed.

Driving Tractors

One morning the Machinery Officer, Charlie Reed, came to the hostel and said to me "You're down for tractor work, aren't you?" When originally signing on there was a choice of jobs – such as milking and dairy work, tractors, field work, rat catcher and horticulture, not forgetting our sisters in the Timber Corps. I'd opted for general field and tractor work, so Charlie said "Come with me, I've got a job for you". Taking me in his van to Theddingworth village, we went into a cornfield that had been started on with the combine. Two men were there, Harold Moore and Sid Gamble, both were repairing the combine. This was before we had self-propelled combines. There was also a Caterpillar tractor. "There's your tractor. Learn to drive it," said Charlie. This particular type of tractor moves on tracks and has no wheels or steering wheel and only gear levers. Charlie climbed on the tractor and explained to me how to work it. Then he said "I think you've got it. Keep going round the field as though you have the combine behind you until its repairs are finished". This I did but said "I thought Eileen was on this tractor" to which he replied "Yes, but she made a mistake on the corner coming back too sharply and ran straight into the

The Caterpillar tractor Pat drove frequently in 1945.

cutting bed of the combine, hence the repairs. It frightened her so much she dare not drive it again." So I got the job.

Harold lived on the north side of Leicester and I lived on the south. He was in charge of the combine, so each morning he would come to the hostel to pick me up and take me to work with him. Harold had a huge motor bike. There were no helmets in those days (today's health and safety people would have a fit). We finished this one particular field, cleaned and sheeted down the

combine and were ready to move. The farmer, Jim Rhodes, was so pleased with us that he gave us a tip. Mine was a ten shilling note, which was a lot of money in those days. When I had time to shop I bought a book with the money, written by a local author Mr John Fothergill, who kept the "Three Swans" hotel in Market Harborough.

On we went to a large field up Foxton Road, owned by Mr C. Ashton. Harold had gone on ahead to tell them I was on my way to join them. Fortunately there was a

Harold Moore, the author and Peter Hawkes seated with two unknown men standing.

large space opposite the gateway for me to go through and this was handy for turning my huge monster. There was Mr Ashton and his men waiting for me. It did not take long to unsheet and get down to work. Harold was a health freak and a lovely chap. He would strip off to the waist and bare feet, even in the stubble, which would be very sharp and hurtful. I myself would have on my breeches and gum boots, shirt etc. and a scarf to cover my hair, hopefully to keep clean.

Driving the tractor on our way out to another farm near Kimcote, we were going through Husbands Bosworth, and there being not so much traffic in those days, people came out of their houses to see what was going by, as there was so much noise and rumbling with my tractor tracks and the monster! When I got to the appointed place it was to find three combines there already, so you can imagine the size of the field. There were about eight German POWs to deal with the corn which went into hessian sacks. These days there are blowers on the combine so the corn can be blown up the spout onto the waiting high-sided trailer. Whilst we were there the Labour Officer came to see us; this was about 3 p.m. on a Sunday afternoon. He came to see how we were getting on with the job, saying he was very pleased with us. I said, "May I ask a favour then?" "Yes," he replied. "Can we knock off then? I've worked seven days a week for six weeks, I've a load of washing needs doing." He said "Yes you can." Harold, though such a nice man, never wanted to pack up and indeed on one occasion stayed the night in the field sleeping under the now silent combine. We finally finished this field and had to go into the next field. I said to Harold "I'll never get the combine through that gateway" to which he replied "Unlock the tractor and go and knock the gatepost down." I did have a go. I should have gone at a faster speed for impact but instead found my tractor climbing up the post, so I had to back away quickly! Needless to say Harold went at top gear and soon had the post down, then back to work again. Harold and I stayed together all summer until we were no longer needed. He went off home to work at another agricultural war depot. I was given a four-furrow plough and set to work ploughing, still with a Caterpillar.

Charlie would pick me up from the hostel in his van, coming back to pick me up from work in the evening. I always had to sheet the tractor down under its tarpaulin, never knowing what time Charlie would arrive to pick me up. He turned up one evening saying "Come on, I'm in a hurry, got to be somewhere else." I told him, "You'll have to wait a few minutes to allow the exhaust to cool off before I cover it." "Oh get it done, I want to be off," So sheeted down, just got to the field gate, I don't know why but I turned and looked back, to see a fire on the tractor. The tarpaulin was alight. Fortunately Charlie had an extinguisher in the van and it was soon put out. I took off the cover telling Charlie "That's what you get for being in a hurry." He told me one day he had asked a girl to take two sets of heavy rollers to different farms in Husbands Bosworth, instructing her to get into bottom gear when she got to the top of Saddington Hill as it was pretty steep and twisty. This she did, but the rollers were so heavy that the weight of them pushed her forward. Charlie thought she would never negotiate the small bridge at the bottom of the hill, so he followed to see if she was safe. She finally managed it but at great speed.

On Leave in London

I was due for some leave and one time Violet, Henry and I decided to spend our week in London. We had been saving hard for this. We went along to the station in our uniform buying a return ticket. We had a job to get on to the train as it was packed with service people. However, we finally arrived at Paddington Station having no idea where to go for a room or hotel. We WLA girls were not allowed to use NAFFI canteens, so seeing a Toc H room in the corner of the station went to see if they could help us (Toc H was founded for promoting Christian fellowship). The gentleman there kindly gave us an address just two streets away. This was run by people belonging to the church. Though basic it was nice and clean with good food. We were shown to our room and after unpacking our clothes we went for a walk around and decided to go to a variety theatre in the evening.

I cannot recall the name of the theatre, but arriving there found a queue of ticket holders. We enquired at the box office, but no more tickets were available. Violet and I stood a few moments trying to decide that we should do. A lady, her husband and two teenagers overheard us talking and came over to us, saying "We have two spare tickets, would you like them?" "Yes please," was our reply. They refused to take any money for them. Maybe it was because we were in uniform. We had a lovely evening after all, laughing at Arthur Askey, the comedian, who was very popular at the time.

The next day, coming along near the station, I asked a policeman if he could direct me to the airbase at Eltham. As I mentioned earlier, my sister Gladys was in the WAAF, now billeted there on a balloon site. We followed directions and arrived there to find a guard on the gate. I told him I was looking for my sister and gave her name and number. He phoned through to the office and a few minutes later Gladys came along. We were given a cup of tea and Gladys explained to the officer who we were and, seeing us also in uniform, gave Gladys forty-eight hours leave.

This was lovely since she knew her way around London and was able to show us some of the sights as well as the ruins and rubble. We went to Lyons Corner House for lunch. This was the first time I had eaten asparagus. My sister was able to have a single room at our hotel which was nice and suited all of us, especially Gladys as she was getting extra leave.

Whilst in London the first buzz bombs came over. Their correct name was 'V1' and they were launched from France and Belgium by the Germans. It was reported that they were responsible for the deaths of over six thousand people.

All too soon it was time to go back to the hostel. We said our cheerios to Gladys and boarded a train for Market Harborough.

A Visit to the Dentist

One day I was back at the hostel a little earlier than usual. Miss Corner asked me if I would go with Nancy Israel to the cottage hospital in Market Harborough. Nancy has been 'discing' in a field nearby. These discs are rows of heavy metal circular blades which cut up the soil. Nancy had stood on the footplate at the side of the seat and slipped backwards, hitting her head on the sharp blades. I took her to the hospital and we had to wait for the doctor to come. I left her there saying that I'd call back for her. I was due to have four teeth out at the middle top. I was working with Italian POWs at the time and had said to the nice dentist I would feel embarrassed working with men with front teeth missing. He had told me about a new way of making a false set and inserting the new ones straight away after extraction. I thought I'd go to see if they were ready whilst I was in town. He said, "Yes, I'll take the four teeth out now if you like." After that I went back to pick up Nancy. We both arrived back at the hostel – Nancy with a bleeding head and me with a paper towel across my mouth. What a sight! I was reminded that I went with Nancy to visit her dentist one time and there were a lot of stairs to his room. I was whistling and the dentist, Mr Dewey, said "A whistling woman and a crowing hen are neither good for mice or men." Cheeky blighter!

At a much later time Nancy asked me to go with her to visit the vicar in the village as she wanted to get her banns of marriage arranged and she was very apprehensive about going to see him at the vicarage, which was at Tower House next door to the church of All Saints. Nancy and I got along fine together and still remain friends.

THE AERODROME

The aerodrome was just behind the hostel along Foxton Road (adjacent to the present-day Gartree Prison). One farmer told me he had lost 190 acres to it in building it, and other farmers also had to lose land to make way for the 'Drome'. The 14th Operational Training Unit was stationed at the airfield from 1943–45, flying Wellington Bombers. I believe 62 aircrew from this unit died whilst training. You can imagine the impact this development had on a small sleepy village and the surrounding area.

Between Lubenham and Theddingworth was Papillon Hall, 'Papillon' being the French word for butterfly. Here were billeted firstly English soldiers and later Americans. With the airfield and the forty girls at the hostel, Lubenham became very busy. The village had two pubs, the Coach and Horses and The Paget Arms. The latter was owned by Lord Paget who lived along the Laughton Road at Lubenham Lodge. We girls, if not staying in, would go to one or the other of the two pubs in the evening and play either darts or skittles with any of the boys. Dances were also held about three times a week in the Women's Unionist Hall, as it was then known. Today it is the village hall.

Three of us were working in a field next to Sulby airfield where three airmen were repairing a Wellington. I asked if we could have a photo taken with the plane. "You're not supposed to be this side of the fence," said one, but allowed us to take a photo which I still have and treasure. We had to be in at certain times each night, but occasionally obtained an extension for something special. We were invited to a dance up at the aerodrome and had a late pass until midnight. There were two sisters from Nottingham at the hostel, and one of them had a lovely singing voice. At the dance they had a large dance band and a young girl got up to sing. She didn't want to leave with us but we had to run to get in on time. She was just enjoying herself but come Monday she was reported to the

Leicester office and dismissed. It seems a shame but the Warden had forty girls to look after. It couldn't have been an easy job. We also had Christmas parties at the hostel in spite of rationing and these were very enjoyable.

The author, Margaret Bottom, Millie Crew and friendly RAF men at Sulby airfield.

THE AMERICANS

Once when working out at Cranoe haymaking I looked up, and shouted to the others, "Look! Look!" The sky was full of American soldiers descending by parachute, dropping in ours and surrounding fields. They were part of the 319th Glider Field Artillery Battalion, 82nd Airborne Division, training for D-Day. They were billeted at Papillon Hall, known locally as "Pamps" Hall. These men arrived early February 1944 after recently fighting in Italy. It was in the Paget Arms I met Staff Sgt Leroy Peterson. A group of us were chatting and Leroy asked to see me again. I agreed. They were a lovely and polite group of fellows. We had some good times with them, many on a purely platonic basis. We would walk into Market Harborough to the Ritz Cinema on Northampton Road (now demolished). We were standing in the queue when a fellow walked up right to the front, but one of the GIs said "Hey there, come back and get in line. Why do you think we are waiting?" If the Ritz was full we would try for the Oriental Cinema on St Mary's Road.

Papillon Hall from an old postcard.

If the weather was fine on a Sunday afternoon perhaps half a dozen of us would walk to Foxton Locks, a couple of miles away.

Walking along Foxton Road one evening Leroy asked "What's that growing in that field?" I said that it was corn, meaning wheat. "No, it isn't," he said. So we had a friendly discussion about this and he said, "I will tell mum to send us some corn." Of course he meant corn on the cob or maize of which we had no knowledge then. His mum already sent me parcels and in one

American and RAF men drinking in the forecourt of the Paget Arms in about 1944. Courtesy Leicestershire Museums Service.

The table top carved with names formerly in the Paget Arms and now in the Coach and Horses, Lubenham. Photograph Bob Trubshaw.

package along with nylons, slippers and perfume were two corn cobs. One was the yellow maize we have got to know and the other an Indian corn looking like lots of coloured beads. It was lovely! Leroy's mother asked for my mother's address and sent her food parcels which were greatly appreciated.

One time we girls were invited to a party at The Laurels, a large house on the edge of the village. This had been taken over by the US Army medic boys. We could take a partner and so Leroy went with me as we were by now very good friends and getting serious about each other. We had records and dancing with a lovely buffet. It was the first time I had eaten gammon and pineapple together, which was practically unheard of in England. Pineapple never reached us during the war along with oranges and bananas. I really enjoyed it and still it is one of my favourites when I go out for a meal. We got on well with the fellows. One chap named Milton Eddie Weidner asked me if I would go to Leicester with him. He was married and had a daughter almost my age and wanted to send them some gifts, so as Leroy was on duty until evening I said "Yes." So off we went, had a look round, had a coffee and shopped. We went into a large expensive shop down towards the clock tower. Admiring a bracelet he asked the assistant "How much please ma'm?" I forget the price asked but Milton replied "Gee ma'm, I only wanted to buy the bracelet, not the store." I shall never forget him and always have a chuckle to myself when I think of that day.

A lot of people carved their names on one table in the 'Paget Arms' and a Paul Bean is there from USA, as are many others. Some talented fellow had carved the RAF on it, and two different people had carved 'AA', the All American badge. My name is on it along with many others. When the Paget Arms was no longer a pub, Miss Tarry who lived there had the legs taken from the table top, the latter being varnished and framed and hung on the wall. A lovely memory. This carved table top is now in private hands.

One day we girls were at work threshing, opposite 'Pamps' Hall. The guard on the gate was Leroy, as he was not off duty he couldn't come over to us, so we went over the road and got a photo taken by the gate. Leroy asked me to marry him. I said, "Yes. We'll talk about it when you come back." They were about to be shipped to France, or rather flying over and being dropped by parachute. I was writing to Leroy each day; going into the pub for skittles etc., or a sing-along if someone played the piano. Some of the older USA fellows hadn't gone fighting, they were in the stores or cookhouse. One night having a drink with them, one chap said to me "There is an officer coming in here tonight, when he goes out, you follow him as he wants to talk to you." I said OK but this American, Bob, said "Promise me you'll come back in," and I did so. The officer was waiting for me and told me that Leroy was dead, having been killed the second day in France. "Really I shouldn't be telling you this as you are not family." As my letters were piling up at Pamps Hall, the fellows said if he did not tell me they would. I went back into the pub, a bit later excused myself and went back to the hostel, to bed where I had a good cry. The forewoman heard me, came and asked what was wrong. I told her and she fetched the warden who was very considerate and asked me if I would like a transfer, to which I said, "No," as all my friends were here. One day coming in from work, I saw an American airmail letter waiting for me. It had the name Peterson on it and all I could think of was that it was from Leroy, there had been a mistake. But this was not so, it was from his mother asking lots of things about him. She also wanted to keep on writing to me and sent lots of photos of the family in later years. After the war Leroy was taken home and buried in their local cemetery. I have photos of the funeral and his grave.

Life has to go on and so does the work.

The End of the War

I was haymaking with some girls on Sutton Road, Market Harborough in a field next to the sewage works when the manager came and told us that the war in Europe had ended. Of course we were all pleased at this news but we still kept on working. At a later date there was a victory parade in Market Harborough. We girls had not done any marching as we were at work early and finished late. One of the girls was going out with a very nice RAF warrant officer, so we asked him to drill us which we did around the village. Came the day of the parade, he arranged it so that he could call his men to halt. We were three or four groups further back. He then brought us to a halt and were placed at ease. We did not disgrace our

uniform, although Elsie told me later that she heard one old farmer say as we marched by "Look at 'em! God bless 'em! They're rolling around like a load of sheep." It's the first time I've been likened to a sheep!

A detachment of the Women's Land Army parading through the Square in Market Harborough to celebrate Victory in Europe Day, 13th May 1945. Courtesy Leicestershire Museums Service.

Elsie, the author, Ruby, Brenda and unknown girl outside the Paget Arms in 1948.

I don't remember who organised it, but a dance was arranged at the Assembly Rooms in Abbey Street (which is no longer there). This was for all agricultural workers and girls from other hostels, along with German POWs who were now allowed out in the evenings. I was sitting with my mates when one of the Germans opposite got up and came across towards us. Bowing, he asked me to dance. Whilst we danced he asked, "Your name is Pat?" "Yes," I replied and he said his name was Fritz and he was one of the Germans working with the corn when I was combining. I must have made an impression for him to remember me. I occasionally worked with one POW called August Diestal and we'd often meet him when we were cycling to work. At the end of the war the Germans were moved for repatriation from the Farndon Road Camp to one, I think, in Shady Lane, Leicester. One day as I came back to the hostel the forewoman said "There's a large parcel for you in your cubicle." It was more than a parcel. It was a wooden tea chest containing a lovely lamp in the shape of a gas lamp, with two figures beneath representing the song 'Underneath the Lamplight' or 'Lili Marlene.' There was also a jewel box, beautifully carved in wood with a rose on top of the lid and a large wooden tray with two squirrels carved on. There was also a workbox, which extended for easy access to the six drawers within. One of my daughters now has the workbox. They had been made by August, who had been in the German Navy as a ship's carpenter and he certainly knew his trade. Later, when he was back home I received a very nice letter from

The tray, jewel box, workbox and figures from the lamp –
all made by a German POW. Photographs by Bob Trubshaw.

him thanking me for being a friend and saying that he and his wife were emigrating to the USA.

Before the Germans arrived at the camp on the Farndon Road, the Italian POWs were there. One of the Italians, a Sergeant Dante, had a lovely voice and Sylvia, who was a Catholic, told me that he was singing

Thanksgiving Day parade 1945, The Square, Market Harborough. Courtesy Leicestershire Museums Service.

solo in their Catholic church in Market Harborough. Although I was C of E, I decided to cycle into town to join in their service, just to hear him singing. I worked with him on different farms, as, like the WLA girls, the POWs were sent where needed. I was not aware he knew my surname but after they had been moved to be repatriated I received a postcard from him. It had a view of Italy and he wrote saying "Could I show you my country on my way home?" I received four postcards in all from different parts of Italy. How nice!

The Post-War Years

The winter of 1946–7 was very cold and hard. One day we girls were told to jump out of the lorry taking us to work, as the lorry could not get up the hill on the icy snow. We got out to lighten the load and then got back into the lorry at the top of the hill and went on to work. The next morning I was going out of the dormitory dressed ready for work. I met Jean saying to her "Hurry up, you'll miss the lorry." She was not ready at all. Jean replied "We're not going as it was not safe what we were asked to do yesterday. The lorry could have slipped back on to us. You and Dorothy Adcock can inform the forewoman," as Dorothy and I had been delegated spokeswomen for them on other occasions. We went to the forewoman and explained the situation. The next thing we knew was that Dorothy and I had been moved to Somerby hostel near Melton Mowbray.

The weather got colder and colder. We were sent to open up a potato clamp and riddle the potatoes. I was put on filling the bags and there were vicious hooks to go through the hessian sacks to hold them on to the riddle. I thought the hooks would not go through the sacks, but hadn't realised they had done. Fortunately they did not go through my thumb. My hands were so cold I couldn't feel them, and had it gone through my thumb I wouldn't have noticed. After Christmas the weather became worse with piled up snow and freezing conditions. On one occasion we helped to

clear the roads with the German POWs. Finally we were told that if we could get into the Leicester office we could have a travel warrant home, as outside field work was impossible. In addition all ablution blocks were iced up so we were sent home for three weeks. Coming

Jean Bale, Molly, an unknown girl and Rene Smith outside the Congregational Chapel in Market Harborough.

back to Somerby I worked a couple of weeks, then I wrote to WLA Leicester office asking if I could be transferred back to Lubenham. I was told there was not a bunk available, but as they were short on kitchen staff they asked if I would help out there and have my own room at the bottom of the dormitory? I agreed but only on a temporary basis. When another girl left, I was given room in the dormitory and was back doing field work again. Dorothy stayed on at Somerby as by now she had met a very nice fellow and eventually married him.

Mixed Farming and a Marriage

My friend Elsie worked quite often along the Foxton Road for Mr Fred Arnold. It was a mixed farm, a little bit of everything including pigs. Sometimes in winter Elsie would stand in the concrete square that held the combustion stove to have a warm when up would go the cries "Phew, what a smell – go and have a bath and change your clothes, then have a warm." Have you ever smelled pig muck? Mr Arnold kept seventy-eight pigs and a boar named Rommel. Elsie enjoyed working there. She and I got on very well. Sometimes I would go home with her to Leicester for the weekend. Another time she would go home with me. Later Elsie met Arthur who lived near her home and started going out with him. Eventually they got engaged and were married on the 3rd January 1948. I was her one and only bridesmaid wearing a borrowed dress! Her first baby (Billy) was born 1st February 1949. I was godmother. We still write or phone each other.

I celebrated my 21st birthday in December 1946 at a dance in the Village Hall at Husbands Bosworth. We cycled to different villages to join in the fun on Saturday evenings, a game of darts, skittles or a singsong. We would have dances also at the hostel, inviting various people. Sometimes standing in the village hall we'd think "Oh he's a nice dancer," and go and say "Excuse me" to his partner. That did not always go down very well.

The Work Continues: Spudding

As I have said, we did all sorts of jobs. Jean Bale and I were sent to work for a farmer in the village, and one job we had to do was spudding thistles and docks. We were given a spud tool each. This had a long wooden handle with a small square blade at the end. Given a hessian sack each we were to go up and down the fields, and upon seeing a rogue plant in the grass we would put the tool under the thistle or dock and cut them out. We put the rubbish in the sack to tip into a pile in a corner of the field, which at a later date would be burnt. I suggested to Jean that we take a couple of ridges and furrows each so we would not be going over the same patch twice. This was OK for a while then I noticed she kept coming nearer to me. I said, "Stay on your own patch," but no, even nearer. I asked her, "What do you think you are doing?" She replied, "It's those bullocks, they keep coming close to me and I'm afraid of them." I shooed them away – they were only being nosey with strangers in their field.

Another day, we were working at Great Bowden and had stopped for lunch. Sitting in fresh straw in the cattle yard along with the Italian POWs something moved in the straw. The boss pounced on it. It was a rabbit. David killed it, passing it to me with a knife, saying "Gut it" which I did, and one of the Italians was very sick, couldn't blame him really as we'd just eaten lunch, but I was used to this job.

Peas and Tomatoes

Once we were working in a field of eighteen acres which was full of peas. We got a gang of local people as well as the WLA girls. These pea pods were all picked by hand, put into small mesh sacks and placed at the bottom of the field. Next morning a lorry arrived to take them to wholesale market. Now of course there is a machine to do the work. It is much quicker but there is a loss of the camaraderie of working in a gang.

There was always something we'd find amusing, and on another occasion Eileen Bennett and I were sent to work at St Mary's Nurseries on Great Bowden Road. It is now a mushroom nursery, but at that time they grew all sorts of salad vegetables. In a couple of large greenhouses we were told to skim off the top soil as the lettuce had already been cut. We had to hoe out the roots and clean up and prepare for a fresh sowing of another crop. There must have been a postal service too, because I definitely remember trimming and packing strawberry plants for posting. We also packed tomato plants and after a while I said to Eileen "Look at my arms. They are covered with spots." A window behind us was open being between the packing shed and the office. A voice said "Who has got spots? Come into the office". Evidently the leaves and stems of the tomatoes can set up a skin reaction. I was given some ointment for the spots after which it soon cleared up.

Working 'Private'

I had worked for Mr David Fox who lived in the village, either at threshing time or perhaps in small gangs for other jobs. One day he asked me if I would work for him all the time. This was termed 'Private Farming.' One or two girls were already doing this, that is living at the hostel but working just for one farmer. The farmers liked this for continuity of work. Knowing the farm they would have regular jobs each day, such as milking, or mucking out the sheds, before going out into the field for other work. They trusted us to get on with jobs without having to be told or shown what to do. He and his father were always nice to work for and decent to us girls, so I agreed if he arranged it with the War Agricultural Committee in Market Harborough. This he did.

There we so many different jobs when you were employed 'private' and this made the work more interesting. David would milk the one house cow for family requirements. The milk was put into shallow pans and left to stand. Next morning the cream was skimmed off the top to make butter. This was done at his parents' house. I would bring the calves out to suckle from the other cows, and put fresh bedding in for them and a bit of hay in the racks, as well as putting calf cake in pans and water in buckets. Then I would muck out the cow shed, swilling down the floor, and lay down fresh bedding.

Ploughing

Later on I was given the job of tractor man and quite enjoyed the challenge. When I was ploughing at his father's farm in Great Bowden, I had worked a piece of ground setting out another stint. I ploughed up and down a few times and then noticed a dark patch which I had not seen before. I continued ploughing another two or three times, with the patch enlarging all the time. I then got off the tractor to inspect it and realised I had cut into a water main that fed the cattle troughs. I informed Mr Fox who in turn got in touch with the Water Board. So, a few people in nearby cottages were without water for a day until repairs had been done. As I said before it was mostly grassland in this area, also ridge and furrow, but since the field had now been ploughed a couple of times for war effort, the ridges were now nearly flattened out so the water pipe had come to the surface. Sometime earlier when ploughing for David in the eighteen acre field, I realised the engine was going but the tractor was sinking deeper into the ground instead of going forward. David sent for the Ferguson tractor mechanic who did not live too far away in the neighbouring village of Fleckney. He duly arrived and after inspection said it was the hydraulics that had gone. He was able to repair this and I then got on with the ploughing.

On another occasion I was ploughing up the grass between the runways on the airfield, as the RAF had now handed back the land to the farmers, and I hit something with the plough shares. The shares were stuck into a trunk of a tree that had been buried when the men built the aerodrome. I could see what I had to do to undo it but I needed help. There were two airmen working on a plane nearby so I asked if they could push this off whilst I started up the tractor engine to work the hydraulics. They did this for me saying, "We've been watching you. Don't you get fed up going up and down the field all day?" I said that I did not as I had to see that the furrows were straight and turn over the soil to cover the grass and I did not get time to think of many other things. David was none too pleased when I finished that particular job as I had broken four plough shares, at a cost of half a crown each! Could I be blamed? For who knows what was buried there when the runways were built. I had also hit several bags of cement and bricks from old farm buildings that had been knocked down to make space for the airfield.

Hedge Cutting and Other Work

David was excellent at hedge cutting and layering and weaving the cut pieces through the upright stakes. Often we would work together. My job was to move all the unwanted branches, then clean out the ditches to allow the water to run. Sometimes the boss would want some of the left-over thorns from hedging placed in the ditch to stop sheep and lambs falling in. What was left of the rubbish was burned.

Once, after usual morning chores David and I had gone up the fields as a lorry was coming for a load of bales of straw. The weather was foul, raining stair-rods! By the time we'd finished the loading, we were soaked to the skin. The driver went off with his load to Derby. The boss said, "I don't know about you but I'm going home to change." He suggested I go back to the hostel and do the same. So having put my wet clothes in the boiler room to dry, I charged back to the farmyard to do indoor jobs. There was always something to do such as brushing down walls and sometimes whitewashing them. On this occasion I started up a small engine that had a short belt going to a hopper with rollers inside. I put in the oats which would go through rollers and emerge into a large zinc pan as rolled oats. Later I put large mangolds in the hopper, then, unfortunately, this had to be done by turning the handle yourself. These would go through cutters that sliced these into pieces like very thick chips, and would be fed to bullocks in winter along with cattle cake.

There were two pigs at the farmyard, something else I had to see to. These were fed on scraps from the house along with bran. Later in the autumn they would be butchered and the women at the house would salt them in lead troughs, later hanging them up from the beams in the kitchen.

Market Day

Tuesday was market day in Market Harborough. Most of the animals were walked there by nearby farmers. In Lubenham there was a pond and cattle and horses would walk through it on the way to the town, having a drink as they did so. It could be a difficult job getting the animals to market. Often I would be in front, pushing my bike, having to keep a wary eye open, as so many people left their garden gates open, especially on Welland Park Road. Then they would grumble if cattle got into their gardens. Having delivered the animals, I would cycle back to Lubenham and continue my jobs.

I liked the sheep. On a regular basis they would be penned up for inspection and often they would be put through a disinfectant footbath. All lambs' tails were docked when small and the male lambs were castrated. They would also have to be tagged, that is taking off all muck from their backsides to keep them clean and free from flies.

Baking and Bread Rationing

We had a baker in the village who lived near the village green. This was Mr William 'Bill' Pateman. He had a pony and trap which enabled him to deliver bread around the villages. The government decided that bread would have to be rationed, and Bill decided he was too old to have to bother with bread units and form filling, so he gave up baking. This was a great loss as I'm told that before the war not many people owned ovens and they could always be seen on a Sunday morning wending their way through the village to Pateman's, carrying a roasting tin covered with a cloth. The tin held the Sunday joint (if they were lucky enough to have one) surrounded by roast potatoes and Yorkshire pudding, to be cooked in Bill's bread ovens. His wife Flo made her own bread of course. I was able to sample this on several occasions as Bill came to work for David and often asked us in for a cup of tea as we wended our way home after work. I usually had a slice of bread and butter with my cup of tea which was delicious. At work most men had a bottle of cold tea, as flasks did not become widely used until later. If Bill ran out of drink he would go to the twenty-acre field where there was a natural spring. He would fill up his bottle with the spring water, which was always nice and sweet. It didn't harm him as he lived to a very ripe old age!

Potato Picking

We also did plenty of potato picking. It was a back-breaking job. We filled hessian sacks which would be put on a trailer and taken to the edge of the field to be put into a potato clamp. These would be covered over with straw, topped with soil at a good depth, and kept for winter usage. When the camps were opened we had a huge riddle on a wooden frame. We had to use certain size mesh riddles at different times on instructions from the 'War Ag.' The small potatoes would drop down into tin scuttles and go for hen and pig food. The others were graded on top of the riddle for selling to the wholesalers and then to the public.

The Hostel Closes

We girls were told that the hostel was to close by Christmas 1948. We had held parties at other Christmas times but this was a bit special. The kitchen

The final Christmas party in 1948.

staff cooked a lovely dinner, with all the trimmings as some of the foodstuffs were becoming a little easier to obtain, though still rationed. One or two of us volunteered to serve the meal. We had a nice time, said our 'goodbyes' to all, and then went home for Christmas.

David wanted me to stay. Mr Ashton also wanted Frances to stay, and my cubicle mate, Eileen, did not want to go back home. So Mr Ashton offered us three one of his cottages on The Green which was empty. There was a cold water tap outside but we didn't fancy going out there each time we needed water, so he had the water directed into one of the three ground floor rooms and a sink placed there. David bought us an electric cooker and we had a wall built dividing the room. Now we had a small kitchen and a flush toilet in the other small room. This was better than going out in the dark to an old wooden privy. We divided the chores between us and this worked very well. One farmer said he needed help on his farm and David suggested one girl to him but the farmer said that he'd rather have two girls and they could share a room. He ended up with Betty and Jean. Betty lived in Leicester and would go home at weekends. Jean was from much farther north, so she came to me at the cottage at weekends, as her boss John was unmarried and would not have just one girl in the house. We than settled down, to our work and now and then I would have a weekend off to go home.

New Lodgings

Mr and Mrs Simon kept the Post Office and local shop and were very kind to us girls. Now and then if we hadn't gone home, they would invite the three of us round on a Sunday evening to have a little supper and listen to records. Life continued like this for twelve months, then Mr Ashton said he wanted the cottage back. As now some of the forces were coming home, he needed it for his man Jack. Eileen who had been working at St Mary's Nurseries did not want to go back into a factory, so went to Worcestershire

working in horticulture. Frances went back to Leicester. After touting round the village looking for lodgings one couple said they would have me for twelve months. After this the bedroom would be needed as they would have to separate the children, a boy and a girl. Thus I was able to continue my work.

The Cadenza Café. Courtesy Leicestershire Museums Service.

Some Local Characters

There were plenty of characters in the village. One lady used to smoke a pipe, as did another lady near Sulby. Adam, the gypsy, lived in his ramshackle tent along Pear Tree Lane. In the season he would pick watercress from the brook in Foxton Road and sell it to the shop. He was a well-known figure and with his dog 'Bulger' walked for miles around the district. There was Mr Christopher Perkins, an eccentric gentleman whose family at one time owned half of Lubenham village. Many people called him 'Jesus' as he always dressed in a tatty old caftan or skirt, and with his long hair and beard did look very much a religious figure, but he was harmless and always acknowledged you.

The Cadenza Café on St Mary's Road in Market Harborough was owned by Mrs Robinson. She was always very good to our girls. We would go to the counter and ask for a pot of tea. If they were very busy we would be told to go to the kitchen and help ourselves. In the kitchen was a table full of different sized teapots. You would make your choice. You'd be given tea, then left to get your own hot water, food etc. We would pay up at the counter. How nice it was to be trusted!

Weddings

As I have already mentioned, Elsie married whilst still at the hostel. So did a few more. Nancy married Tom Satchell who lived just across the road from the hostel. Maria Sullivan married Jim Perks, also a village fellow. Some of us were invited to this wedding to be held in Leicester. She was a Roman Catholic and Jim C of E. Off we went. Jim was already in the church. We sat and sat and finally Jim was called to the vestry. Being from different religions they had to have a registrar present. The original registrar had forgotten and gone off to play cricket, so everyone had to wait until someone else could be found. Poor Maria was still sitting in the car! We all trooped out of the church and some local people very kindly brought us out cups of tea. Can you imagine; it was like a street party. However, the wedding did go ahead much later!

Joan Goodhew was engaged to Sid Coleman when she came to the hostel. Sid was in the paratroopers and he was later taken prisoner. When released after the war he came home. Eight special friends, including us, were invited to the wedding. We all attended in uniform and formed a Guard of Honour for them. Nancy Miller from Glasgow later married John Gilbert, a farmer's son from Lubenham.

Towards the end of 1949 David and I started going out together. We got engaged at Christmas and married at the beginning of June 1950. This had to be fitted in between turning the bullocks out to grass from their winter yards and haymaking.

Quite a few of our girls married and still live locally.

The Women's Land Army Society

The Women's Land Army Society was founded a few years after the war, which enabled us to take part in a number of functions. One was to visit the Imperial War Museum to see an Exhibition of Agriculture which included the WLA and a meeting with the then Minister of Food. In 1995 we WLA girls were invited to the VE and the VJ celebrations fifty years on.

David and Pat on their wedding day in 1950.

In 1996, Prince Charles, having seen the WLA on parade, kindly invited us to Highgrove House. Invitations were sent to us and we went in three coaches. When we arrived at the gates, the police with sniffer dogs checked the coaches. We then split up into four groups, were shown round the gardens by guides and were taken to have tea on the terrace but which turned out to be a really wonderful buffet tea in a beautiful large marquee. Prince Charles arrived in his red helicopter. He came into the marquee and shook hands with every one of us. He was quite prepared to stop and chat here and there, and accepted a photograph from me of himself and other members of the Royal Family when they visited Thorpe Lubenham Hall and attended the Lubenham Church in the 1950s. The Queen Mother was our patron through the War and she has since attended one of our reunions in Birmingham. In recent years, the WLA has been included in the muster at the Royal Albert Hall Remembrance Service. The year 2000 was the first time the WLA paraded past the Cenotaph for the wreath-laying ceremony.

In the time I was in the WLA in Lubenham, I lived at six locations in the village, all of which are within a quarter of a mile of the WLA hostel where I lived when I first arrived in April 1943. These included the house David and I live in now.

Though many of the girls, I'm sure, felt it their duty to join one of the women's forces, for us working on the land became a labour of love. It was a love of the animals, the countryside and joy in the crops as they matured and were harvested. It must have been so, for over five thousand women stayed to work on the land when the WLA was disbanded in 1950.

The war completely changed my life and I made so many lovely friends who I will never forget. Bless 'em all!

By this personal message I wish to express to you

MISS PAT SMITH

my appreciation of your loyal and devoted service as a member of the Women's Land Army from

29th APRIL, 1943, to 18th MARCH, 1950.

Your unsparing efforts at a time when the victory of our cause depended on the utmost use of the resources of our land have earned for you the country's gratitude.

Elizabeth R

Postscript

In recent times the government has officially recognized the magnificent work that the Land Girls contributed to the war effort. In 2000 former WLA members were allowed for the first time to join other armed forces veterans on the Remembrance Day march to the Cenotaph. In July 2005 the Queen unveiled a bronze sculpture of women in the war next to the Cenotaph in Whitehall. It is a permanent tribute to the contribution made by seven million women during the 1939–45 war.

Finally in January 2008 DEFRA (Department for Environment Food and Rural Affairs) acknowledged the tremendous efforts of the Women's Land Army and Women's Timber Corps by presenting their surviving members with a specially-designed badge commemorating their service and acknowledging the debt that the country owes to them.

Some further reading

'Alex' (1993) *Graips and Gumboots: Memories of the Women's Land Army*, SMI and RSH.

Bates, Martha (2001) *Snagging Turnips and Scaling Muck: The Women's Land Army in Westmorland*, Helm Press.

Cole, Pauline (2001) *Transition to Arcady: A Story of Two Years Spent in the Women's Land Army – '47 to '49*, Arthur H. Stockwell Limited.

Davies, Ross (1975) *Women and Work*, Arrow Books.

Dean, Marjorie (1995) *The Women's Land Army and Me*, The Pentland Press.

Duggan Rees, Josephine (2000) *Corduroy Days: A Portrait of Life in the Women's Land Army*, Woodfield Publishing.

Gryspeerdt, Mary (1993) *Back to the Land: The Story of the Women's Land Army in Somerset*, Friends of the Abbey Barn.

Hall, Anne (1993) *Land Girl: Her Story of Six Years in the Women's Land Army, 1940–1946*, Ex Libris Press.

Hardie, Melissa, Ayres, Diana, Butler, A. (2006) *Digging for Memories: The Women's Land Army in Cornwall*, The Hypatia Trust.

Harris, Carol ((2000) *Women at War 1939 – 1945: The Home Front*, Sutton Publishing.

Hill, Maureen (2003) *Britain at War: Unseen Archives*, Paragon Books.

Powell, Bob and Westacott, Nigel (1997) *The Women's Land Army in Old Photographs*, Sutton Publishing.

Sackville-West, Vita (1993) *Women's Land Army*, Imperial War Museum.

Shaw, Do (2002) *Back to the Land (Oberon Modern Plays)*, Absolute Classics.

Tillett, Iris (1988) *Cinderella Army: Women's Land Army in Norfolk*, I. Tillett.

Tyrer, Nicola (1997) *They Fought in the Fields: The Women's Land Army – The Story of a Forgotten Victory*, Mandarin.